A MESSAGE FROM NFIB'S PRESIDENT, WILSON S. JOHNSON

In 1978, William E. Simon wrote the excellent *"A Time for Truth."* In his own candid manner, Mr. Simon told us what he learned during his years of service in Washington. He pointed out why private enterprise in America was in trouble and told us what could be done to get us back on course. We at NFIB were so impressed with that book that we arranged for each member to have a copy of the Reader's Digest condensation.

Now, Mr. Simon has written another book, *"A Time for Action,"* which is as important to small-business people as *"A Time for Truth."* That is why, again, we are making copies available to you.

"A Time for Action" suggests that while the election of President Reagan was a major step toward reversing the trend of more than 20 years of big government, it was only the first step. In this book, William Simon tells us what we can and must do as concerned Americans to restore the personal and economic freedom which are the lifeblood of our free enterprise system. I hope you will read—and heed—the message this book contains.

Sincerely,

Wilson S. Johnson
President
NFIB Research and
Education Foundation

WILLIAM E. SIMON

A TIME FOR ACTION

DISTRIBUTED BY
NATIONAL FEDERATION OF INDEPENDENT BUSINESS
RESEARCH AND EDUCATION FOUNDATION
150 W. 20th Ave.
San Mateo. CA 94403

Berkley books by William E. Simon

A TIME FOR ACTION
A TIME FOR TRUTH

A TIME FOR ACTION

An Enterprise America/Berkley Book / published by arrangement with
the author

PRINTING HISTORY
Reader's Digest/Berkley edition / October 1980
Enterprise America edition / November 1981
NFIB Research and Education Foundation edition / December 1981

ISBN: 0-425-05732-1

A BERKLEY BOOK ® TM 757,375

PRINTED IN THE UNITED STATES OF AMERICA

Foreword

Six weeks before the election of Ronald Reagan, I published the first edition of *A Time for Action*. In it, I described the tragic policies which had combined to saddle the American public with double-digit inflation, rapidly declining productivity and intolerable unemployment.

In his first ten months in office, President Reagan has made great strides toward restoring America's economic vitality. Major cuts in federal spending, substantial tax reductions and long-overdue business deregulation have been achieved against great odds. But much more remains to be done—and can be done only with the full support of the American people.

To help mobilize that support, I offer this extensively revised, updated and condensed version of *A Time for Action*. It is dedicated to my fellow countrymen with the fervent belief in their ultimate wisdom and with the passionate hope that they wake up before it is too late.

William E. Simon
October, 1981

I.

Controlling the Leviathan

On November 4, 1980, the American people assessed the damage inflicted on the nation by years of collectivist misgovernment and delivered a thundering verdict at the polls.

The election of Ronald Reagan and a sharply more conservative U.S. Senate signaled the culmination of one process in our politics and the beginning of another. What culminated was the growing disenchantment of the American public with shopworn practices generally called "liberal" but which in their devotion to big government and hostility to individual freedom are in fact illiberal and reactionary.

What *began* was a painstaking effort to restore America to the path of greatness from which it had been derailed by more than a generation of excessive government. By creating an opportunity for such restoration, the election of Ronald Reagan was a marvelous beginning. But it is crucial to stress that it *was* a beginning and that years of work and struggle remain before our liberties are once again secure.

The federal government of the modern era spends far more money and exercises far more power over our daily lives than our founding fathers could possibly have envisioned and far more than the average citizen of the present hour can possibly imagine. And, driven by the dynamics of the welfare state psychology, that spending and the accompanying power have been expanding at a giddy rate that is equally hard to fathom.

In the 25 years since 1956, the federal government has spent more than $6 trillion. Three quarters of this total —$4.5 trillion—has occurred since 1970, and half of it— $2.9 trillion—has occurred since 1976.

The rate of increase is even faster for social welfare— the largest single component of government outlays. Since 1956, federal spending in this category has amounted to $2.4 trillion. Eighty percent of this has been spent since 1970, and 57 percent of it—or $1.3 trillion—since 1976.

This is much more than the "growth" of federal spending; it is a veritable explosion.

In tempo with this mammoth hike in spending, the scope of federal regulatory power has increased as well—particularly in the past decade. In 1970 the *Federal Register* containing rules and regulations promulgated by the bureaucrats amounted to 20,000 pages. In 1980 the number had grown to 87,000 pages—and in the last two days of the Carter Administration contained more than ***1,000 pages daily***.

The end result of all this spending and government regulation, most observers are now willing to admit, has been a cataclysmic failure. We have created such an enormous and costly burden of government spending, taxes and regulation on the home front that we have crushed the productive vigor of the economy while feeding the fires of runaway inflation by excessive increases in the supply of money.

Simultaneously, we have seen a drastic weakening of our national posture overseas. Despite the constant outcries that we hear about the "military-industrial complex," the truth is that we have actually financed our recent binge of domestic handouts by siphoning money from essential military needs.

In the past generation, as measured in constant dollars, federal spending for all purposes has more than doubled, increasing by 116 percent. Social welfare spending, measured in this fashion, has grown by ***531 percent***, while spending for defense has grown by *0.4 percent*—which means it really hasn't increased at all.

The concomitant decline in our defenses—and in the conduct of our national policy overseas—is discussed in more detail in the succeeding pages.

In his first year in office, President Reagan has made a courageous start toward grappling with these problems. In his economic program, he has gone far toward restoring confidence in the integrity of the dollar and refurbishing incentives for individuals and businesses through his tax and budget package.

In addition, the Administration moved rapidly on the deregulatory front—lifting, modifying or postponing hundreds of "midnight regulations" hammered together in the closing hours of the Carter Administration and moving to alleviate the consequences of hundreds of others.

What Reagan accomplished in this span was in fact nothing less than a counterrevolution in our politics. Using his superb ability to communicate, he broke the political dominance of the Keynesian economists, reorienting the national debate to such essential topics as productivity, incentives, hard work, savings and deregulatory initiatives to free up the powerful creative energies of the American economy.

In the realm of foreign policy, the Administration has sought to base our conduct on a solid, factual understanding of the Soviet adversary. Early policy stances on the neutron bomb, El-Salvador, conflict in southern Africa and the need to refurbish our defenses are in refreshing contrast to the vacillating conduct of the past few years.

Major attention has been focused on the President's economic program, and properly so. But much of what is said about this program is incorrect—and could lead to a mistaken perception of what remains to be accomplished.

It is widely stated, for example, that the President's program has involved "cutting the budget." In fact, to hear the yelps from the affected interest groups, you would think that the budget has been slashed back to the bone. To get a more accurate picture, consider that the revised federal budget for fiscal '81 produced by Jimmy Carter in March

1980 indicated total outlays of $611 billion.

Slightly more than a year later, the so-called "austerity budget" pushed through a reluctant Congress by President Reagan for fiscal 1982 amounted to over $720 billion—$100 billion *more* than the Carter projection for '81.

What in fact was happening here was a reduction in the rate of increase of the budget—not the actual size of it. That rate was slashed back from 13 percent a year to about five percent—a needed step but hardly the decimation that the illiberal liberals and the handout specialists would have us think.

Much the same was true with respect to the Reagan tax cuts. In fact, the rate reduction sought by the President was a *rollback of tax increases* programed into the economy by the combined effects of inflation and progressive tax rates. As people get pushed into nominally higher income brackets, their tax rates go up even though their purchasing power doesn't.

As Senator William Armstrong (R., Colo.) put it: "Taxflation pours so much additional revenue into the federal Treasury each year that almost all of President Reagan's 25 percent income tax rate cut was required just to keep taxpayers where they were. If Congress had rejected the Reagan tax and spending cuts, most Americans would be pushed into the 50 percent bracket by 1990."

In both these cases, the President sought to slow and eventually turn the graph lines which show the federal government absorbing an ever larger percentage of our Gross National Product—a procedure examined in more detail in Chapter IV.

In both cases also, the President boldly tackled what I call "government on autopilot"—the process of automatic spending and taxing hikes that the illiberals have so thoughtfully built into our system. On the one hand, added revenues flow into the Treasury through "taxflation." On the other, billions flow out through so-called "uncontrollable" entitlement programs such as food stamps, unemployment compensation or Medicaid, triggered by external economic factors rather than Congressional decision.

"Taxflation" will now be brought under control through indexing, but the automatic spending process remains—constantly driving budgetary totals upwards and making mincemeat of the official forecasts. Clearly, these "uncontrollables" must be brought under restraint—for political as well as economic reasons.

Viewing the huge deficits engendered by this runaway spending, there really is no mystery to the sky-high interest rates that have afflicted our economy. Those rates are the inevitable effect of runaway inflation and public expectation—born of sad experience—that it is going to continue. Nobody wants to lend money at ten percent if he thinks the inflation rate is going to be 12 percent; that's a negative rate of return, even before the taxes that must be paid on purely nominal interest income. The inflation rate is a *floor under the interest rate,* and as inflation zooms ever higher, so does the cost of borrowing. A generation of cumulative deficits compounded by constant expansion of the money supply—supposedly meant to keep interest rates down—has managed to drive them constantly higher.

Our economic problems have been created by interlocking errors of fiscal, monetary, tax and regulatory policy, geared to the mistaken notion that we can get something for nothing through the top-down manipulations of federal planners. We have now moved to correct our tax and regulatory problems, and the Federal Reserve under Paul Volcker has tried to hold the line against reckless expansion of the money supply. But we have yet to get our fiscal house in order.

As long as we permit federal spending to balloon through "uncontrollable" entitlement programs, outlays are going to run ahead of revenues, with the resulting deficits "crowding out" private borrowers and driving interest rates still higher. (In the period 1975–81, federal deficits averaged more than *$60 billion a year,* sopping up one quarter to one half of the available credit in our economy.) Inflation is our number one domestic enemy, and unless we bring federal spending and deficits under control, it will eventually destroy us just as it destroyed Weimar Germany, China before the communist takeover and postwar Hungary.

As important as the economic impact of such policies are the *political* effects of runaway federal spending. As long as the "uncontrollables" hold sway, vital decisions about the scope of federal spending and government incursions on private freedoms are made without effective input from—or knowledge by—the voting public. This is a complete inversion of our free political system, which is supposedly based on popular sovereignty.

This usurpation is equally glaring in the realm of federal regulation—as unelected bureaucrats crank out a myriad of rules and guidelines with the force of law, affecting the most vital interests and concerns of the American people. The average citizen whose will is supposed to be sovereign in our system has no effective knowledge of this process, much less decisive influence over it.

In all these respects, the task confronting the Reagan Administration and the country can be summed up under a single heading: ***To reclaim control of the political system, the economy and the freedom of the average citizen from the elitists who have created all this enormous power and who, because so much of it is insulated from popular authority, still exercise tremendous influence on national policy.***

The pages that follow sketch out the nature of the Leviathan that the President is attempting to combat and the forces that are arrayed against him. I think the impartial reader will agree that, while the Administration has made a noble start, it is ***only*** a start, and that much remains to be accomplished.

For those who believe in the traditional values of personal freedom and limited government, the 1980s will truly be a decade of decision. It was just 200 years ago, in the decade of the 1780s, that the American experiment in liberty was legally and constitutionally established, leading to the greatest saga of human accomplishment and abundance known to history. The challenge of our era is to renew the faith, and reclaim the wisdom, that made America the greatest and freest nation in the world.

II.

The American Crisis

Three years ago, I wrote a book about my experience in the federal government *(A Time for Truth).* For someone whose life had been spent in the business and financial world, my tenure in Washington had been a harrowing and depressing experience. A sadder but, I hope, wiser former Treasury Secretary, I thought the outlook for our economy and the global situation was bleak. I didn't know the half of it.

In that previous book I described the forces of envy, greed, political blindness and ideological arrogance which, in my view, were leading our country toward a double form of perdition: collectivist regimentation on the home front, weakness and prostration in our dealings overseas. A nation governed in this manner, I concluded, had a rendezvous with oblivion. After I wrote that analysis, all the tendencies that disturbed me accelerated.

The graph lines pointing toward economic collapse for the nation zigzagged crazily off the charts, signaling "May Day" to anyone who had the slightest knowledge of commonsense finance and economics. In our foreign dealings, the signs and symbols of our weakness were piled on with ever more humiliating frequency.

In early 1980 inflation rose to an almost incredible annualized rate of 18 percent—a figure previously thought appropriate only for banana republics. At this clip, our money would lose half its value in only four years' time.

In a frenzy of speculation in 1979 and '80, gold prices soared to more than $800 an ounce, up from $42 in 1971. Which is another way of saying that the present and prospective value of the dollar, in the eyes of those prepared to pay such prices, had fallen by an equal magnitude.

In the summer of 1979, for the second time in five years, motorists on the Atlantic and Pacific seaboards found themselves snarled in monstrous gas lines or confronting "Closed" signs at their local service stations. This in an energy-rich nation where two thirds of all the discovered oil remains in the ground, where tens of billions of recoverable reserves are waiting to be extracted and where coal, natural gas and nuclear power resources are immense.

Numerous mortgage institutions closed their loan windows in 1980 as mortgage rates soared above 15 percent. *Three quarters of the American population found themselves priced out of the new housing market, and the housing industry, with the lowest number of starts since World War II, was in a state of virtual collapse.*

Housing wasn't alone. In the past few years, once mighty U.S. industries—electronics, steel, automobiles—have been staggering toward disaster, unable to meet the challenge of foreign competition. In 1979 the nation's 17th-largest corporation, Chrysler, came hat in hand to Washington to seek—and get—a federal bailout.

In 1979 business productivity in the United States declined by 1.7 percent. By the middle of 1980, after dropping for four straight months, industrial production was lower than it had been in 1978.

Between 1979 and 1980 the average earnings of American families, in terms of purchasing power, decreased by more than five percent. (A nominal gain of eight percent in income was more than countered by a 13-plus percent increase in consumer prices.)

In May of 1980, despite a tremendous gusher of federal spending and countless programs supposedly intended to create jobs, the number of new unemployment claims soared by the highest level in our history—675,000 in a single week. Americans thus continued to suffer the unique experience of "stagflation"—simultaneous inflation and recession.

As of the end of 1979, total debt in the United States, public and private, had reached the staggering total of $4.25 trillion. Default on any substantial portion of these colossal obligations could trigger a banking panic of frightening dimensions.

The list of economic horror stories could go on and on: our massive trade imbalance; $180 billion in federal deficits in four years; continued declines in capital investment. *It is incredible but true that over the past 20 years the United States has the worst record of capital investment of any major industrialized nation in the world.*

Since investment is the key to productivity—which must improve if our standard of living is to increase—this shortfall affects our ability to compete not only in global markets but in our own. And without sufficient investment, there cannot be jobs for our growing labor force—or for our children.

Steel is a good example. In 1955 we exported more steel than we imported. But sweeping government regulations and de facto price controls affected investment and productivity so adversely that between 1964 and 1977 our growth in output was exactly zero. The Japanese, meantime, have increased production by an average annual rate of 14 percent. Markets, profits and jobs for American steel are disappearing: 100,000 jobs for U.S. steelworkers were lost in a single decade.

Multiply that record across a host of other industries and you have some idea about the frightening nature of our problem. Key aspects of our economy have been grinding down toward zero, while rampant inflation has pushed money prices toward stratospheric levels. *Until President Reagan was able to push his budget and tax rate cuts through Congress, the projected outcome was a declining standard of living, the continued loss of jobs, more government intervention, higher inflation and the ultimate prospect of financial panic and collapse.*

If we turn our attention to the foreign scene and what has happened to our nation in dealings with other countries, we find a series of events that, if anything, is even more appalling.

In September 1979, 3000 Soviet combat troops were "discovered" in Cuba. President Carter and numerous other high officials in our government repeatedly said this situation was "unacceptable." On October 1 the President went on national television—and accepted it.

In November 1979 a third world dictatorship in Iran, led by a religious fanatic, sacked our embassy and took 53 Americans hostage. A single furtive attempt at rescue by our government ended in humiliating failure in the desert. (The hostages were finally released January 20, 1981 in obvious response to the arrival of a no-nonsense President, Ronald Reagan.)

In recent years, other American embassies and consulates have been attacked in India, Afghanistan, Bolivia, Colombia, Turkey, The Netherlands, Luxembourg, Syria, Lebanon, Libya, Pakistan and other countries. In the past decade, according to CIA and State Department estimates, more than 600 personnel abroad have been subject to attack. In Afghanistan our ambassador was murdered; in Colombia he was kidnaped; in El Salvador he was held prisoner in his residence.

In December 1979 Soviet troops rolled into Afghanistan—using vehicles provided to them by American policymakers and American industry. We responded with mostly symbolic gestures, the most serious of which were soon retracted. The Soviets, predictably, ignored these feeble

protests and kept right on murdering Afghan peasants.
(*Their* embassies, for some reason, don't get taken over by
third world countries.)

***All authorities agree that the decline of the U.S. military
had proceeded to a point where we were second in striking
power to the Soviets.*** The Secretary of Defense, in fact,
informed Mr. Carter that we lacked the capability to project
enough military power into the Persian Gulf to back up our
warnings to the Soviets. Our state of strategic readiness is
so poor, according to one survey, that we would be better
off not to respond to a Soviet strike against our missiles,
since retaliation would only incur additional strategic pun-
ishment.

Our conventional readiness is dismal. A U.S. Army exercise indicates that 90 days into a conventional war we
would be more than a million men short of demand and in
some critical areas would have only 30 percent of trained
manpower requirements. Skill levels among the men we do
have are abysmally low (90 percent of the soldiers main-
taining our nuclear weapons failed their skill qualification
tests).

These examples too are culled from a long and dismal
list. We could add such further signs of national weakness
as the handing over of the Panama Canal, our vital linkage
between the two great oceans, to the late dictator Omar
Torrijos; the subsequent efforts of Torrijos and his mentor,
Fidel Castro, to bring a Marxist regime to power in Nicaragua, with the acquiescence of our State Department; and
the use of Nicaragua, again with our compliance, to launch
aggression against El Salvador and Guatemala.

As with our domestic troubles, these foreign calamities
are symptoms of a deeper process unfolding steadily across
a span of decades. Anyone who surveys the changing map
of the world can see at once what is occurring. The United
States and its allies have been in headlong retreat, while the
Soviet Union and its proxy forces around the world have
been steadily advancing. After a generation of relative stale-

mate, the past few years have seen ten different countries taken over by the Marxists,* and others are being threatened as this is written. These conquests are significant not only because they show the general drift of power in the world but because they provide the Soviets and their allies with crucial leverage over global resources and strategic choke-points. Angola and Mozambique command important sea-ports vital to world shipping; Afghanistan and South Yemen are pincers around the Persian Gulf; Nicaragua is an alternative to Panama as a site for an interocean canal and moves the Marxists closer to the huge oilfields of Mexico.

While the aggressive ambitions of the communists are not within our power to control, the question of whether those ambitions succeed or not is powerfully affected by what we do—or fail to do. The effective stalemate that lasted from the Korean War until the early 1970s occurred because the communists feared the strength of the United States and because we pursued a set of policies designed, for the most part, to stem the Soviet advance. *In recent years, this perception of our strength—and of our will—has changed dramatically for the worse.*

Like our domestic economic troubles, these foreign policy woes are largely self-inflicted. When the world sees us back down on Soviet combat troops in Cuba, or unable to prevent a Persian fanatic from holding Americans hostage, or handing over a vital waterway under threat of sabotage and riot, they conclude that we lack the guts and will to stand up for our interests. And when they observe that we cannot pull off a military rescue mission, or that it takes two weeks to get a carrier to the Persian Gulf, they also conclude that, even if we had the will, we haven't got the means.

Both conclusions have been right—and both are results of self-created weakness. The decision to accommodate ourselves to third world Marxist revolutionaries has been

*South Vietnam, Cambodia, Laos, Angola, Mozambique, South Yemen, Ethiopia, Afghanistan, Nicaragua, Zimbabwe Rhodesia

the result of a deliberate policy in Washington; so has the decline of our strategic and conventional defenses. Add the buildup of the Soviets by systematic transfusions of our technology and the ripping apart of our intelligence agencies by Senate demagogues and media zealots, and the recipe for disaster is virtually complete. We have been weak and pusillanimous in our foreign dealings because of what we have been doing to ourselves.

I am frightened by what has happened to my country, by the forces which have ravaged our economy, by the record of weakness and capitulation in our foreign policy. Still, I believe the basic character and constitution of the country are sound and can survive—but only if economic and foreign policy quackery is abandoned.

A major part of the problem is the sheer enormous size of the federal government. The central government has grown to such monstrous proportions that it has sucked the lifeblood from our states and local communities, profoundly changing the nature of our federal system. But at the same time, it has become so huge that it is often beyond the control of *federal* officials—at least the elected ones. To a degree that the average American only dimly comprehends, it runs according to its own momentum.

It is this enormous, rudderless federal government that is the basic source of our economic problems, i.e., runaway spending, confiscatory taxation, oppressive regulation, as well as the resulting intolerable inflation, which have crushed the life out of our economy.

It is because of this gigantic burden that we have been experiencing declining investment, falling productivity, staggering industries, energy shortages, chronic unemployment and runaway inflation. The American economic system is a willing steed, but even the strongest beast of burden will collapse if too much weight is piled upon its shoulders.

Even more important, this massive and mindless government intrusion has threatened the most precious of our worldly holdings—our personal freedom. Not only units of state and local government but private institutions and individual citizens have discovered they cannot conduct the business of daily living without getting the permission of "Big Brother"—the incredible alphabet soup of bureaucratic OSHAs, EPAs, DOEs, EEOCs, FTCs and other regulatory agencies.

Even after the budgetary and tax rate reductions won by President Reagan, our government is much too big and powerful—far more so than our founding fathers could possibly have envisioned. Yet at the same time, this government is much too weak.

Our system, after all, is not supposed to be anarchic. Our founders believed government was a necessary institution in society—to provide for the common defense, maintain internal order, see to the administration of justice. These functions are essential to freedom because they neutralize the aggressive use of force that threatens the life and liberty of the individual.

Yet these functions—particularly those pertaining to defense—have been performed inadequately or not at all by the self-same federal government that presumes to regulate the minutest aspects of daily life.

The federal government has been massively strong where it should be restrained, pathetically weak where it should be strong. We have a federal government that has told us how our toilet seats should be shaped but could not prevent our embassies from being sacked or our citizens from being taken hostage.

I believe the disorders of our times are, in several senses, the product of a spiritual as well as an intellectual crisis. The troubles we experience are the result of a contagion that affects the whole of our society—political leaders, intellectuals, businessmen, average workaday citizens. *We have been without direction, ultimately, because we have lost the compass bearings of religious faith and patriotic affirmation. Only if we know what we believe, and why we believe it, can we chart a successful course back to recovery.*

III.

Me the People

Most issues in our politics today are discussed in terms of "conservative" and "liberal" philosophy, as if the problems before our nation are things that only ideologues can understand or care about. That way of approaching the matter, in my view, is totally mistaken. Arguments about political philosophy are well and good, but the issues confronting America today are far more basic than any fine-grained disagreement over theory.

What we are talking about is a matter of survival. We are talking about whether human liberty around the world is going to be destroyed, whether we are going to follow rules of simple prudence in our domestic economic policies.

On fundamental issues of this type, there is, or ought to be, a broad consensus. Opposition to seeing our fellow citizens locked up and pushed around by foreign dictators is hardly a matter of ideology. I don't know of any political viewpoint in this country—beyond the lunatic fringe—that favors totalitarian dictatorship over human freedom. And neither liberals nor conservatives—nor anybody in between—want the United States subjected to a foreign enemy or destroyed in a nuclear attack.

Whatever our political point of view, the need to survive in freedom is not a subject for debate. It is no more necessary to engage in highbrow discussion about these matters than it would be to convince someone he shouldn't throw himself under a speeding truck or jump out of an airplane without a parachute.

In dealing with such questions, we urgently require some simple common sense. One rule that most of us learn from childhood is that if somebody is trying to do you harm, you better keep your guard up. There are plenty of somebodies out to get us in the world today, and they have spelled out their goals with total clarity. *By their words and actions, the communists in Moscow and elsewhere have made it plain that they intend to bury us.*

They have been saying so for years, and there is no reason to suppose that they are kidding. The foremost task of the American government is to protect the nation and its people from this determined onslaught.

A second rule we learn from childhood is not to invite attack through weakness. Nothing encourages a would-be bully more than the belief that his intended victim is unable or unwilling to resist. Trying to buy off a bully by giving in will only prompt him into pushing harder. That's the kind of treatment America has been getting at the hands of Moscow and numerous other, lesser tyrants.

On the domestic side, the rules are equally straightforward. There is no free lunch. You can't spend yourself rich. It is impossible to consume what is not produced. America's industrial might and widespread affluence weren't built on high-toned economic theories but on certain fundamental values: self-reliance, thrift, hard work, initiative, willingness to take a risk, readiness to accept the consequences.

The common theme of our recent failings is a headlong flight from these essential values. We have tried to live in a fantasyland where we can have our cake and eat it too. We have wanted peace and freedom overseas without fac-

*ing up to swaggering bullies who make destruction of peace
and freedom their full-time business. And we have wanted
the fruits of a productive economy without investing the
patience, work and sacrifice that generate all economic
progress.*

Never in the history of nations has a weakened country
internally been able to maintain a posture of strength ex-
ternally. America's weakness domestically has meant America's weakness abroad. While the government was accu-
mulating power in Washington over its own people, it was
losing the power to influence events elsewhere in the world.
As our economic position deteriorated, so did our military
and diplomatic positions and our leverage as a global leader.

Consider the decline of the dollar in global markets. This
was in part a strictly economic phenomenon—a judgment
by holders of our currency about the miserable way we have
managed our economy. That verdict is bad enough, but
falling confidence in the dollar is also a political judgment
on our republic. *When a nation's currency goes into decline, it signifies not only weakness on the home front but
weakness internationally.*

A nation's currency is an emblem of its sovereignty.
Great nations have historically exerted leadership not only
through the power of their ideas (which is always primary)
but by the strength of their economies, the soundness of
their currencies and the standard that these provide to others.

*Apparently we have bought the idea that rules applying
in individual cases somehow get suspended when we are
dealing with collectivities. It's a bad policy for an individual to give in to a bully, take somebody else's property,
live beyond his means or sacrifice future benefit for short-
term gain. But somehow these notions become transmuted
into statesmanship when practiced by the government.**

On the domestic scene, a veritable crusade has been

---

*Adam Smith understood the problem better. "What is prudence in the
conduct of every private family," he said, "can scarce be folly in that of a
great kingdom."

waged by Keynesian economists to convince us the rules
of ordinary logic do not apply to government: Chronic debt
may be bad for an individual but is good for a nation.
Savings and thrift may seem desirable in individual cases
but are bad for a country. The constant preaching of such
themes has served to make illogic and extravagance seem
respectable.

This short-term strategy leads inevitably to long-term
problems. As the extent and size of federal handouts have
expanded, the burden of taxes has become prohibitively
high. And people who want the handouts don't want the
taxes. Presto, another easy answer: deficit spending—which
keeps the subsidies high and the taxes (to outward appear-
ances) low.

*Deficit spending does not eliminate the costs of gov-
ernment. It only conceals them. Everything in life must
be paid for somehow, and we are paying dearly for our
deficits: a national debt of $1 trillion, interest charges of
$100 billion a year and rampant inflation spurred by fed-
eral pressure on credit markets and an irresponsible expansionary monetary policy.*

A variation on this tunnel-vision view of politics is the
eagerness of legislators and regulators to adopt one-shot
"solutions" to problems without concern for the remoter
consequences of such action. In the legislative arena, this
generally takes the form of adopting some subsidy or en-
acting some program that will allegedly address a current
crisis, without any clear assessment of what the costs will
be in terms of taxes, inflation or other burdens on the economy.

The most extreme version of this is the attitude of some
environmentalists and consumerists, who demand that any
perceived problem be banished, instantly, with no weighing
of costs. What these campaigns are saying is, we demand
Utopia—now—and don't care how we get it. Such attitudes
would be more appropriate in a permissive kindergarten
than in the councils of a once-great nation.

The politicians have created all this, but the public has permitted it—even demanded it. It is hard to think of an interest group that hasn't come clamoring to Washington in recent years requesting subsidies, protection, and regulations conferring competitive advantage.

We know about the ripoff artists in the welfare, food stamps and CETA programs. But I've come to the conclusion that many businessmen aren't much better. They're worse, in fact, because they above all others should appreciate and defend the values of free enterprise and self-reliance. Yet all too often they seek bailouts, federal favors or regulatory protection from competition.

As our "me the people" psychology spread and became pervasive, all our weaknesses intensified. We communicated the message that everyone has the right to live at the expense of somebody else; that consumption has no connection with productive work; and that if people are careless, lazy or incompetent—whether they be businessmen or food stamp clients—they will be bailed out by Washington.

The net result of such an approach must be, and has been, to discourage thrift and enterprise and to encourage evasion of responsibility.

An appropriate symbol for what is happening to our nation might be Peter Pan—and I don't mean peanut butter. Our desire to achieve immediate gratification, avoid responsibility and have others care for all our needs is like nothing so much as infantile regression.

And that, not too coincidentally, is exactly how "Big Mother" down in Washington has too long thought of us: as children who cannot be trusted to think for ourselves, plan for the future, insulate our homes, operate our power mowers or do anything else that grownups should be capable of doing. We have been treated as helpless, self-indulgent infants who need a federal nanny to look after us at every waking moment.

A people that demands perpetual handouts and regulatory coddling inevitably makes big government bigger.

A government that takes over all the responsibilities of living must make a people ever smaller. Only if we can break this downward cycle of dependence can the American nation survive in freedom.

IV.

Where Your Money Goes

Most efforts to describe the size and workings of government these days remind me of the blind men trying to describe an elephant by feeling different parts of it—and having no idea of the total immensity of the subject. The only change I would make in this image would be to substitute a brontosaurus for the elephant. But because of this immensity, it is essential that we make an effort to grasp the scope and nature of government activity. Unless we understand what it is doing to our economy, our money and our lives in general, we will be unable to take corrective action. ***The very hugeness we don't understand will eventually crush us.***

Federal budgetary totals, federal deficits and federal regulatory costs these days are all measured in the hundreds of billions of dollars. Such numbers are not only unwieldy, they are basically incomprehensible. Most of us have never seen a billion anything, much less a billion dollars.

Such problems are faced all the time by Congressmen and Senators, who are supposedly in charge of all the spending. In order to make the numbers manageable in their own calculations, they treat $100 million as though it were one dollar. A $300 million appropriation, in budget committee markups, is simply called "three."

This facilitates calculation; it also correctly conveys the attitude toward taxpayers' money that prevails in Washington: $100 million is chicken feed—the lowest possible unit of computation. As Senator Everett Dirksen said: "A billion here, a billion there; the first thing you know, you're talking about real money."

The way they think in Washington was indicated by President Carter when he presented the nation's first $500 billion budget in 1978 and proudly described it as "lean and tight." Because most people have no comprehension of the sums involved, this incredible statement went down like a spoonful of sugar. From the standpoint of most Americans, he might just as easily have been talking about $500 trillion. To understand what is really involved at this colossal level of spending, it may prove useful to break the arithmetic down to more manageable proportions.

If you had started out at the birth of Christ spending $700,000 a day, every day, with no time off for weekends or holidays, and had simply continued spending money at that rate through all the intervening centuries, you would just recently have succeeded in getting rid of $500 billion. Or, to put it in a shorter time frame, to spend this much money in a single year, our government had to disburse nearly a million dollars a minute ($951,000) around the clock every day of the year. That worked out to $57 million an hour, or $1.37 billion a day.

As shocking as the absolute size of the federal budget is the direction in which it has been headed—straight up. We are so used to hearing these huge spending totals tossed around that it seems things have always been this way. They haven't.

Ninety percent of this huge growth of government has occurred in the past ten years. In fact, the budget grew as much in the last two years of the Carter Administration as it did during the first 175 years of our nation's existence.

If we simply look at the official spending totals as a share of national output, we discover that in 1930 government at all levels was taking about ten percent of gross national product. By 1980, it was taking 36 percent of GNP. Moreover, it has been calculated that if we had simply kept on doing what we had been doing, extending the growth curve across another 20 years, government by the year 2000 would be taking 67 percent of GNP.

As bad as all this sounds, the total government burden on our economy is a lot bigger than the officially acknowledged numbers. Add in so-called "off-budget" items (including federal loan guarantees and borrowing by government entities) amounting to an estimated $60 billion a year, $120 billion in regulatory costs imposed on the private economy and tens of billions of federally mandated outlays by state and local governments, and it is likely that federal activity, right now, is imposing a cost of nearly $1 trillion a year on our economy—out of a nominal GNP of $2.5 trillion. This is pure dead-weight cost on the productive sector of the nation.

Most of this tremendous spending increase has been for domestic subsidy programs—not, as we are frequently told, for the "military-industrial complex." It is calculated that in the fiscal '81 budget, 53 percent of all federal outlays were for so-called "transfer payments."

A good example is the food stamp program, which started in 1965 with 442,359 recipients and a budget of $35 million. In fiscal 1981 there were 23 million recipients, and the program cost was over $10 billion.

Spending on the program doubled in the last three years of the Carter Administration and increased 1000 percent in the past decade. Despite copious evidence that the program is shot through with fraud, ineligible recipients, etc., Congress resisted efforts at reform and actually loosened eligibility standards. When 23 million people are getting benefits from a program, that's the way the political dynamics operate.

In August 1975 I greatly offended Senator George McGovern (D., S.D.) by charging that the food stamp program was "a well-known haven for chiselers and ripoff artists." When the South Dakotan squawked at the assertion, I was glad to provide more than 100 pages of fine-print evidence documenting fraud, waste and mismanagement in the program. In the intervening years the problem has only gotten worse.

The Department of Energy budget for fiscal '81 also stood at upwards of $11 billion—more than double the combined budgets of the three departments it replaced (so much for greater efficiency) and more than the 1978 profits of the seven major oil companies combined.

To his credit, President Reagan wants to dismantle DOE. But what have the American people been getting for their $11 billion a year? To date, the DOE has not pumped a barrel of oil out of the ground. So what, exactly, happened to all the money? Researchers trying to get an answer to this question received vague responses—which became more understandable when it was revealed that 87 percent of the DOE budget was going to consultants and contractors working on such important projects as energy deskbooks and a solar racquet club in California. All of which is the moral equivalent of pouring money down the nearest rathole—with the difference that the inhabitants of this rathole are waxing fat at our expense.

One of the clearest examples of the incredible ripoff that occurred in the name of combatting the energy crisis was the birth of the "synfuels" industry—which came into being for the sole purpose of scooping up $20 billion in government subsidies. The *Wall Street Journal* reported the lavish cocktail party celebrating the passage of this boondoggle—featuring U.S. senators, regulators and lobbyists smacking their lips at the prospect of such massive handouts. Repeat that scene a thousandfold and you will have some idea of what has really happened to taxpayers' dollars funneled through the federal "problem-solving" machinery.

Using reports from the General Accounting Office and

other agencies, investigative reporter Donald Lambro estimated the waste, fraud and incompetence were costing the taxpayer at least $100 billion annually. Examples of the ridiculous spending that go to make up this composite figure are endless, but some of the choicer ones have been assembled by Senator William Proxmire (D., Wis.) in his Golden Fleece Awards. These include:

• Expenditure of $57,800 by the Federal Aviation Administration to study body measurements of airline stewardesses (for safety purposes);

• $1 million disbursed by the Environmental Protection Agency to preserve a Trenton, N.J., sewer as a historical monument;

• $120,000 from the National Highway Traffic Safety Administration to build a special motorcycle that no one could ride, and so on in profligate absurdity.

Waste is built into a system where billions of dollars are tossed around in reckless fashion with little oversight by Congress. Lambro cites the Smallpox Division of what used to be the Department of Health, Education, and Welfare, which has a well-paid staff and research budget of $1 million annually—even though smallpox has been extinct in the United States since 1947. The total lack of accountability for such programs is suggested by a Senate staff aide who commented on the Foreign Claims Commission:

We just don't have time to look at agencies like this. We have to be concerned with much larger subjects—SALT, the Panama Canal treaties, China. We have to let agencies like this one go by the board.

The difficulty the average citizen has in understanding all this is made worse by deliberate efforts at concealment by the bureaucrats and their friends in Congress. A typical sleight-of-hand technique is the "consultancy" dodge, used to cover up the tremendous growth of federal employment. As the government expands its role, it simply hires "consultants" or creates "independent" corporations and agencies to disburse the dollars and conduct the studies, staffed by people who don't show up on the official manning tables.

Count in all these consultants and other invisible federal payrollers and the true number of employes is between 11 and 14 million rather than the 2.8 million officially acknowledged.

As federal spending totals have risen, so have annual budget deficits and the rate of inflation. The parallel is no accident, and it is one of the most frightening and potentially ruinous of the many incredible things we have been doing to our economy.

The fact that we have been caught up in a runaway inflation is known to everyone. In 1979 the consumer price index rose at an annual rate of 13 percent. In the first quarter of 1980, prices went up at an annualized rate of 18 percent. People found the buying power of their dollar shrinking toward the vanishing point, savings accounts eaten up, mortgage interest rates going sky high. Those on fixed incomes are hardest hit by such gyrations, but the harmful effects are by no means limited to these unfortunates.

It wasn't too long ago that various Keynesian double-domes were telling us a little inflation was good for us and that we could easily sustain two percent or even five percent annual inflation rates. Unfortunately, the "good" effects of inflation—making people think they have more real income when they only have more paper dollars—tend to wear off as soon as price levels rise to equal the increase in purchasing power. This requires another dose to get the "good" effect again—at a higher level.

Our inflation record over the past 20 years shows this effect clearly: from 1960 through 1964, the average rate was 1.5 percent; from 1965–69, 3.5 percent; from 1970–74, 5.8 percent; and from 1975–79, 7.1 percent. And for the past two years we have been well into the double-digit regions, compounding on top of what has gone before.

Compound interest has been described as the eighth wonder of the world—when it's working for you. When it's working against you, there are few things more lethal. And chronic inflation makes compound interest work against us with a vengeance. It is rapidly destroying the purchasing power of the dollar and value of pensions; it is silently robbing U.S. taxpayers of billions of dollars; and it is fatally undermining our ability to maintain a productive economy in an increasingly competitive world. Over the decade of the '70s, inflation increased at an annualized average rate of almost seven percent.

The result of this inflation rate, compounded, was to cut the purchasing power of the dollar by 50 percent. People who retired on pensions in 1970, therefore, had their purchasing power cut in half.

Business Week points out that at an annual inflation rate of eight percent (well below what we have recently experienced), a worker who leaves a job with vested pension rights at the age of 45 will lose 80 percent of the pension's value by the time he is ready to collect it. The horror story gets even worse. Professor Dwight Lee of Virginia Polytechnic Institute observes that, should recent inflation rates prevail for another generation, someone now earning $20,000 would have to earn $1,280,000 just to stay even. And shortly after the turn of the century, a $1 hamburger will cost $32, a $10 shirt will cost $320, a $25 pair of shoes will cost $800, a $5000 car will cost $160,000 and a $75,000 house will be selling for $2,400,000.

President Carter argued that the culprit is the rising cost of energy imposed by OPEC. To see the fallacy of this, we need only note that major industrial nations which are even more dependent on imported oil than we are have inflation rates about one third our own.

The real reason for our inflation is that the federal government in recent years has been running enormous deficits and expanding the money supply to help pay its bills. To ease the pressure, the Federal Reserve System creates more credit in the form of deposits for the Treasury—in effect, creating money and injecting it into the economic system. That's inflation.

According to Lord Keynes, Lenin said the surest way to destroy a capitalist economy was to debauch its currency through inflation. Chronic inflation confuses and disorients people as they search for someone to punish for their misery. Hyper-inflation sets workers against employers, businessmen against consumers and housewives against grocers in a constant round of angry bickering. This social effect is one of the worst results of inflation—and one that grimly fulfills the scenario laid down by Lenin.

A government as huge as this is a far cry from the original design of our founders. Madison said the powers of the central government under our constitutional system were to be "few and defined." This was to be a system of limited government, with the central authority checked by the reserved powers of the states, in the interest of protecting individual freedom. Today we have a central government whose powers are the opposite of "few and defined" and which, far from being limited by the states, treats them as financial dependents and administrative serfs. President Reagan's heroic efforts to transfer authority from Washington to the states are long overdue, but it is indeed ironic that they are opposed by many governors and mayors who have become addicted to the narcotic of federal funding— and control.

V.

America on Autopilot

Our government is supposed to be representative of the people speaking through their elected legislators. It should, however, be apparent that, in a system where Congress doesn't even know about the existence of certain agencies, the operational control of Congress has been weak to non-existent.

Such a loss of control is inherent in a complex regulatory system. There is simply no way that Congress can write up technical occupational safety standards, assess the purity of the atmosphere, conduct deliberations on pricing levels, inquire into the nature of carcinogens or do the thousands of other things the regulators say need doing. *As a result, the unelected bureaucracy became the de facto lawmaking power.*

The trend was unmistakable in the *Federal Register*, the daily compilation of rules and regulations issued by the bureaucrats for the governance of our businesses, work conditions, products, schools and homes. It was in those pages, which quadrupled during the past decade, that the actual "Law of the Land" was written.

Symbolic of the trend toward totally unaccountable government is the widespread practice of talking about "uncontrollables." By one recent estimate, 77 percent of federal outlays are in this category—meaning outlays triggered automatically by age, economic conditions, income status or other factors extraneous to the political decision-making process.

Medicaid, unemployment compensation and food stamps are examples. Calling such things "uncontrollables," of course, is just another cop-out, since all such programs are created by laws which can be changed. But the rhetorical twist helps spread the notion that big government runs itself, constantly getting bigger, and that there is nothing anyone can do about it.

Essentially, the government has been running on autopilot—without the knowledge or approval of the people and with scant regard for their concerns or interests.

As a result of this arrangement, policies have been put in place that are not only different from, but directly counter to, the wishes of the people. Such programs as busing, affirmative action, edicts from the Department of Housing and Urban Development and numerous business regulations from the Federal Trade Commission have reflected not the views of the American public or its elected representatives but the social engineering enthusiasms of a small elite controlling the regulatory process.

By and large, the performance of the major national media obscures the truth of what is going on in Washington rather than revealing it. Examine the issues covered by the big news outlets—and those that aren't covered—and it becomes apparent that media enthusiasms and aversions closely parallel those of the counterculture.

Issues of interest to the crusaders get extensive coverage, pretty much the way the counterculture likes to see them handled. Other issues tend to get ignored. Individuals and groups involved in the crusade are given favorable treatment. Those on the other side are given the business—and I don't mean stock in CBS.

Sometimes the treatment is a simple matter of choosing words to describe people on varying sides of public issues. As Irving Kristol has noted in the *Wall Street Journal, there seem to be plenty of "ultra-conservatives," "right-wing Republicans" and rightward "extremists" reported on TV but hardly any "ultra-liberals," "left-wing Democrats" or leftward "extremists."*

Sometimes the treatment is more heavy-handed, as in the case of nuclear power. This subject combines most of the pet peeves of the counterculture in one convenient package: "hard" energy, corporate enterprise, fueling our industrial machinery, economic growth. The combination is almost irresistible, and stopping nuclear power has become a number one project of Fonda, Nader, Commoner and Company. And in pursuing it, they have been able to rely at every step of the way on the full cooperation of the major media.

The clearest example of such misreporting was the accident at Three Mile Island in Pennsylvania, where the media (aided by garbled statements from officialdom) had the public believing a nuclear explosion was in prospect, that a horrendous "meltdown" with massive radiation releases was about to occur, that a so-called "hydrogen bubble" was going to explode and so on—all of which was totally false. Small wonder the President's Commission on Three Mile Island concluded that the worst health hazard of the episode was "severe mental stress"—induced by false, hysterical stories of an impending holocaust.

Similar misleading stories are fed out on a continuing basis on a host of other subjects of interest to the counterculture—such as the oil companies and their alleged "obscene profits." In fact, you can set your calendar by this one: Whenever the quarterly profit figures for the oil companies show an increase, this gets played in the media in a misleading way that can only convince the American people they are being ripped off.

One of the most flagrant examples of such treatment was provided by a CBS commentator who talked about

"290 percent profits" in the oil industry. It turned out this
was a figure for one company, Amerada Hess, which had
a particularly low profit margin of 2.7 percent in the third
quarter of '78 and managed to raise this to 7.6 percent
in the third quarter of 1979. Thus, an actual margin of
less than eight cents on the dollar was translated into a
"290 percent" increase and, even worse, "290 percent
profits."

Whether such ridiculous misstatements stem from bias
or incompetence is hard to say, but the effect is the same
in either event. Such nonsense is undoubtedly accepted as
gospel by many people and thus serves to whip up antag-
onism toward the oil companies, preparing the way for
punitive legislative and regulatory measures.

Among the worst examples of media misrepresentation
was the recent CBS-TV series on national defense, an alleged "documentary" which relied on research from veteran
disarmament lobbyists to prove that we were spending too
much on the military and was accordingly lambasted in such
publications as *Commentary* and *The Washingtonian*.

The series all too clearly fulfilled the Walter Cronkite
statement of some years ago that "there are always groups
in Washington expressing views of alarm over the state of
our defenses. We don't carry those stories. The story is that
there are those who want to cut defense spending."

Equally indicative of media attitudes was the fashion in
which the Washington *Post* and *Wall Street Journal* relayed
to the American public the researches of CIA defector Philip
Agee, seeking to discredit the Reagan State Department
white paper documenting communist involvement in El
Salvador. Agee has said, "I aspire to be a communist and
a revolutionary," and has made a career of trying to wreck
the CIA. Neither the *Post* nor *Journal* acknowledged the
extent of their reliance on his researches—which would
have discredited the stories with many of their readers.

As all these items suggest, our "right to know," as ex-
ercised through many of the national media, is strangely
selective. We are entitled to endless exposés on such items

as Watergate, the alleged evils of nuclear power, the inner workings of the CIA and so on—exposés often as false as they are relentless. Concerning issues that cut the other way, however, we are given almost no information, or provided with data that are inaccurate.

The issue here, obviously, is more than fairness or unfairness to particular individuals, although such judgments are important. The point is that the media, by such behavior, are warping the political system beyond all recognition.

VI.

The Regulatory Stranglehold

In pressing forward with a comprehensive program of de-regulation, President Reagan understands well that the existing tangle of governmental regulation, allegedly designed to protect the little guy and serve consumers, often does the opposite. In fact, it is almost always those who are *already powerful* who benefit from economic regulation. And there is plenty of evidence that government interference in other areas—health, safety, the environment—has a similar counterproductive impact.

Start with the massive costs imposed by constantly increasing regulatory demands, paperwork requirements, capital outlays for pollution control, etc., etc.—the $120 billion that business has to spend each year in order to meet governmental regulatory requirements. Such massive expenses are not easy for any firm to absorb, but they are obviously more difficult for small firms than large ones.

A good example is the "ERISA" pension reform adopted by Congress in 1974. This bill required business firms offering pensions to their employes to observe procedures and provide benefit guarantees comparable to the largest corporations. Obviously, such requirements were difficult for small companies to meet, and many of these simply terminated their pension plans as a result (7300 plans were abandoned in 1976, an 84 percent increase over 1975).

Similar results followed adoption of the Food and Drug Amendments of 1962, vastly increasing the amount of documentation required to certify new pharmaceuticals. The average cost to certify a new drug under these requirements increased from about $2 million in 1962 to $54 million in 1978. Only the largest of pharmaceutical companies have been able to absorb this burden and forge ahead with innovations—with the result, according to a study from Duke University, that drug innovations have become increasingly concentrated in the larger pharmaceutical houses.

The recent troubles of the auto industry also make the point. While all auto manufacturers are suffering from a combination of economic ills, including excessive government regulation, it was the smallest and shakiest of the "Big Three"—Chrysler—that was the first to go down. Although I am no defender of Chrysler management—and opposed the federal bailout—it is obvious that, because the company had a volume only one fourth the size of GM's, per-unit production costs required by regulation were much higher—$620 compared to GM's $340. To meet GM's price competition per unit, Chrysler had to settle for a smaller margin per vehicle.

What is true of regulatory costs in general is also true of specific types of regulation. *So-called "protective" regulations in the field of transportation, financial institutions, communications, etc., have the effect of guarding developed, powerful interests already in the field and heading off competition from fledgling entrants who might lure business from the big boys.*

Protecting the big guys has been the object of transit regulation from the beginning. As the Interstate Commerce Commission once put it, its policy historically has been "to protect already authorized carriers from unintended or unwarranted competition." The Civil Aeronautics Board once voiced a similar view, asserting: "We recognize that some competition between local service carriers and trunk lines (major air carriers) is inevitable, but we intend not only to minimize such competition but to prevent its development to the greatest feasible extent."* These statements have been fully borne out by experience.

• When the CAB was founded in 1938, there were 19 trunk lines serving large American cities. Forty years later, there were 11. In this span of four decades—a period of explosive growth in air travel and exciting new technological developments in aviation—not a single new major carrier was certified by CAB. Smaller non-scheduled airlines that arose to give competition in the 1940s were relentlessly driven to the wall and limited in the services they could provide. Only in geographically large states like California and Texas were smaller independents able to compete effectively, since CAB authority did not extend to intrastate airlines.

• The Federal Communications Commission has authority over broadcast licensing, allegedly to divide up frequencies and avoid "jamming" of the airwaves. Beginning in 1966, however, it asserted its authority over the infant Cable TV industry—which doesn't use the airwaves and doesn't get involved in "jamming"—to freeze its development in the 100 largest markets in the United States. This move was made strictly to protect the interests of the networks, their owned stations and their affiliates, which as a result enjoyed cartel-like benefits in all these cities. Only recently has the regulatory death grip on Cable TV been relaxed.

• In the middle 1960s, Joe Jones of Atlanta, a black man with experience in the trucking business, applied to the ICC for an operating license to run truck service between the

---

*These attitudes have been altered, I am glad to say, in the last several years by legislative and administrative pressures for deregulation at both agencies.

South and Northern cities. This request was routinely denied on the grounds that existing truck lines were providing all the service that was needed. (After an outcry in Jones's behalf, this denial was reversed.) The turndown was par for the course in trucking regulation—where entry has been strictly limited, routes apportioned on a monopolistic basis and rates collusively set with the approval of the government.

Consider the case of the Big John boxcar Southern Railways tried to introduce in 1961 to permit more efficient and lower-cost handling of grain. Because of the efficiencies of operation that this new boxcar permitted, Southern requested permission from the ICC to reduce its grain haulage rates by 60 percent.

This was loudly protested by the truckers and the barge lines, who didn't want such low-priced competition, and it was only after a four-year battle before the ICC and the courts that Southern was able to get this rate decrease accepted—resulting in lower grain, milk and poultry prices for consumers in its service area.

Where prices in regulated versus non-regulated segments of the same industry can be compared, they are almost always lower in the non-regulated categories. It was found that air carriers operating entirely within the boundaries of California or Texas, and thus immune from the CAB's tender mercies with respect to rates, had fare levels approximately 50 percent lower than those certified by the CAB. Similarly, agricultural commodities carried by truck (exempt from ICC rate regulation) moved at prices substantially lower than those for regulated commodities.

Higher prices are only one of the costs consumers have to bear because of government suppression of competition and innovation. Since the introduction of the 1962 drug amendments, for example, the rate of introduction of new therapeutic drugs in the United States has been cut in half, and the United States, once a leader in this field, now brings up the rear. As a result, many life-saving drugs for treating heart disease, hypertension, asthma and other diseases that are available in England, France and other nations are not available to Americans.

How many people have died in America because drugs useful in treating heart disease available in other countries are not accessible in this country? Dr. William Wardell of the University of Rochester puts the number of coronary deaths at 10,000 a year. Professor Sam Peltzman of UCLA has estimated that the harm inflicted by the 1962 amendments far outweighs whatever marginal good they may have accomplished. It is doubtful that if penicillin were introduced today—or aspirin—either could survive the obstacle course erected by the FDA.

Other counterproductive consequences in the field of health care have followed from federal intervention. Direct subsidy programs such as Medicare and Medicaid and federal tax treatment of health insurance plans have radically tilted our medical economy toward a system of third-party payment—in which someone other than the patient picks up the tab (90-plus percent of hospital bills are handled on this basis, 55 percent of them paid for by the federal government).

Unsurprisingly, in the decade after adoption of Medicare and Medicaid, health care spending went through the roof: Hospital charges rose by 300 percent, while consumer prices generally were increasing by 75 percent. The medical "cost explosion" that the federal regulators then sought to "contain" by bureaucratic fiat was itself a creation of the federal government.

The new "social" regulation favored by the counterculture and implemented by such agencies as EPA, the Consumer Product Safety Commission, OSHA, etc., differs from the old "economic" regulation in that it cuts across industry lines and is characterized by a general hostility to business rather than being captive to some segment of it. That distinction, however, does little to make it more beneficial for consumers. On the track record, in fact, this "social" regulation is just as harmful in terms of price and counterproductive consequences in the realm of health and safety as the old-fangled economic kind.

Housing offers a prime example. There have always been building, safety and other regulations in the housing field. But the past decade has witnessed an explosion of new "environmental" regulations mandating energy standards, specific types of insulation, underground wiring and low-density construction, requiring permits from literally dozens of state, local and federal agencies. This process has increased the capital costs of building and greatly prolonged construction schedules—from a period of months to, now, a period of years. New housing costs, as a result, have increased in geometric proportion.

Because of this regulation—interacting with inflation-driven mortgage rates—the vast majority of Americans has been priced right out of the new home market.

In 1970, according to data compiled by the National Association of Home Builders, 47.7 percent of the nation's families could afford a median-priced new home. By 1979, the number was down to 23.5 percent. This fits the program of the "no-growth" crusaders to a T. As Professor Bernard Frieden has demonstrated, the object of much so-called "environmental" regulation in this area is to freeze out the riffraff by making development standards and costs prohibitively high.

Such crushing economic costs might be acceptable if they were really the price of improving the environment, but there is precious little evidence that this is so. In fact, *a lot of this one-eyed regulation actually damages the environment. The classic case is the ban on DDT, a compound which has saved millions of lives by suppressing disease and increasing agricultural yields around the world and has never, so far as is known, been the cause of a single human death. With the crackdown on DDT, millions of acres of crops and forest land have been stripped by insects, malaria has staged a global comeback, and numerous pesticides have been marketed as substitutes that are far more lethal for human beings (but safer for insects).*

Not counting the costs or consequences of regulatory

actions involves more than dollars and cents. It involves unforeseen impact on health, safety and the environment and economic growth beyond the immediate visible effect of a given action—impacts that the regulators in their blinders-on fixation with single objectives refuse to consider.

The question is not dollars versus lives—but lives versus lives. And the evidence is good that, in addition to imposing enormous dollar costs on the economy, the regulators are actually blighting and destroying lives rather than enhancing or saving them. Again we are dealing with an almost childlike mentality that seeks a quick fix now without considering remoter implications.

VII.

The Great American Seed Corn Banquet

For most of the past decade, the American economy has hardly grown at all.

Any index you care to look at tells the story: Real Gross National Product has been inching forward at a snail's pace; worker productivity per man-hour has fallen to less than a third of its former rate of increase and in 1979 declined; from 1973–79 there was no increase, to all intents and purposes, in output per worker employed in the U.S. economy; and from 1979 to 1980 the purchasing power of the average American family not only didn't grow—it shrank approximately five percent. Wonderful, isn't it?

While the no-growthers in their redwood hot-tubs may be toasting each other with Perrier over these developments, it is doubtful American workers and consumers generally will share in the enthusiasm. The decline in our rate of productivity advance has meant a loss of real income to American citizens—about $3700 less per family in 1978 than if the previous rate of growth (about three percent a year) had been permitted to continue.

41

Economist Ezra Solomon of Stanford states the issue—and the problem—this way:

"Over the past century, each American generation has enjoyed a standard of economic life twice as high as its parents—and we have come to accept this steady improvement as a fact of life. [However,] at the rate of improvement we have achieved since 1973, it will take not one generation but 300 years to double average living standards. At the rate we have achieved over the past year, we will be lucky to maintain 1979 standards."

Why has our rate of economic growth and productivity been declining? There is no real mystery. Simply put, our nation is staggering under the tremendous weight of a government apparatus that absorbs almost 40 percent of GNP and distorts the workings of our economic process with its irrational policies. The combined effects of high tax rates, regulatory costs, government deficits and runaway inflation have caused our economy to grind down to zero. Add the explicit effort of certain elements in our society to *force* a no-growth policy on the nation and the outcome is a foregone conclusion.

Our productivity troubles are simply one aspect of a national passion for living for the present, at the expense of the future—what I call "the great American seed corn banquet."

For any nation that wants to maintain its strength and provide a rising standard of living for its people, the "seed corn" is that portion of its resources it sets aside for growth and development. It represents a decision to forego *present consumption* in order to provide for *future benefits.* It can consist of, literally, seed corn, or time taken to construct a better fishing pole, or a hoe, or buying a tractor, investment in industrial equipment, computers or satellite technology. It is that portion of present earnings set aside to provide for better tools that will enhance productivity.

In our economy, the "seed corn" is the amount of resources we devote to better equipment, research and development and technological and other innovations that permit continued forward movement along the path of economic progress. Such investment in the future in a vast society such as our own requires staggering set-asides—according to one estimate, better than $4 trillion in the period 1974–85 to finance the capital needs of our economy.

Investment on this scale is needed, in the first place, to provide new jobs for our expanding work force. For a variety of reasons above and beyond natural population increase, our labor force has grown enormously in recent years. In the past decade alone, some 18 million new jobs have been provided for American workers. Since it takes more than $40,000 to provide a single job in American industry, the demand for investment capital to handle this continued influx into the economy is obvious. To provide employment for all these people and enhance the living standards of American society generally will require an enormous investment of "seed corn."

If you eat the seed corn, however, you can't plant it. To the degree that we divert resources from savings and investment to the heedless pleasures of immediate consumption, we decrease our harvest. This is exactly what we have been doing in America in recent years.

In May of 1975 I went before the Senate Finance Committee on one of my numerous treks to Capitol Hill to plead for savings, investment and productivity and to warn against the dangers of what we were doing to our economy. I spelled out the record that showed us lagging behind other nations in terms of providing for the economic future, discussed the negative impact of taxes, inflation and regulatory costs and deplored the adverse effects that all of this would have on the health of our economy and the standard of living of our citizens. But not for six years, until President Reagan was able to win enactment of his tax rate and budgetary cuts and begin instituting regulatory reform, was anything done. And the failure to act in that period caused grave damage to a once-vibrant economy.

Over the past two decades, the United States has brought up the rear among industrial nations in percent-

age of Gross National Product held as personal savings.
From 1973–77 other industrial nations were saving be-
tween ten percent (Canada) and 25 percent (Japan) of
GNP. During that same span, the United States saved only
6.7 percent, and in recent months the savings rate has fallen
as low as 3.4 percent.

All investment comes directly or indirectly out of somebody's savings—either private or business—and U.S. investment rates have predictably declined with the fall-off
of personal savings. In the period 1962–78 the United States
ranked dead last among eight major industrial nations in
average investment as a percentage of GNP. Our average
rate was 17.5 percent, barely more than *half* the Japanese
rate of 32 percent. Unsurprisingly, in view of this much
higher investment rate, the Japanese have three times our
rate of productivity increase and a 137 percent higher rate
of growth for GNP.

The results of this shortfall in U.S. savings and investment are intensely practical for those who want to get better
jobs—or hold the ones they have. Because other countries
have been surging ahead of us in savings and investment,
they have also been outproducing us in many industries.
This means their products are bought in other countries in
place of our own—and, in many instances, in the United
States as well.

Electronics, textiles, steel and automobiles are examples
of industries in which we have fallen behind in terms of
technological advance and productivity. This loss of global
markets means loss of jobs. *Business Week estimates that*
the resulting decline in U.S. economic power meant $125
billion in lost production in the 1970s and the loss of two
million plus jobs in the American economy.

In recent decades, the federal government operated what
amounts to a comprehensive program for devouring economic seed corn as fast as it could be shoveled from the
granary. The first and most obvious problem was simply
the amount of resources that our enormous government con-

sumed directly. The nearly 40 percent of GNP being gobbled up by government at all levels was nearly 40 percent of GNP that, by definition, was not available for private savings and investment. This government spending was almost entirely devoted to current consumption at the expense of long-term future planning.

These effects on savings, investment and productivity are almost trivial, however, compared to the effects of inflation. *Chronic inflation, borrowing against the future to finance the political pleasures of the hour, is more than a seed corn banquet—it is a Roman orgy.* The ways in which it destroys capital, discourages savings and investment and decreases productivity are almost too numerous to elaborate. Suffice it to say that if one really wanted a "no-growth" posture for America, the policy of deficits and inflation we have pursued in recent years is enough, all by itself, to get the job done. A few examples:

—When the federal government goes into the money markets to finance its huge deficits, it sops up capital that cannot be used by private business. In recent years this "crowding out" effect has gone as high as 35 to 40 percent of total borrowing in the economy. This pushes up the rate of interest and, as noted, leads to expansionary policies to make sufficient credit available for other borrowers—i.e., creation of new money, or inflation.

—By its very nature, inflation is calculated to discourage savings and investment and to encourage present consumption and debt. If the purchasing power of the dollar is going to be cut in half in a decade, it makes little sense for me to hold that dollar in a savings account. Better to spend it now while it still has some purchasing power left. In fact, it pays me to consume not only everything I have but also what I *don't* have—in other words, go into debt. I can pay back my creditors in the future with dollars that are worth less than the ones I borrow.

—Inflation wreaks havoc with businesses which seek to retain earnings for investment or to attract equity capital.

Tax writeoffs for depreciation become grossly unrealistic under inflationary conditions since replacement costs are so much higher than the historical cost of·acquisition. Profits and resulting taxes are correspondingly overstated, while taxes imposed on capital gains—even at the reduced rate of the 1978 reform—are taxes on inflationary increases and thus amount to a confiscation of capital. (We are one of the few countries in the world even to have such a tax.)

While there have been managerial lapses in some industries, businessmen in general are concerned about future investment. They have to be; unless they make provision for plant improvements and new equipment, they will go out of business. The rate of business savings in our economy has therefore remained relatively constant through the years—despite the inflation and other governmental obstacles—at slightly under 12 percent of GNP. However, so much of this has to be diverted to meet government regulatory requirements and satisfy the demand for inflation-hedging purchases by the public (especially residential housing) that the total amount invested in new and better equipment has been pathetically meager. Professor Michael Boskin estimates that in 1979 real net addition to plant and equipment actually amounted to less than two percent of GNP. This works out to approximately $40 billion or roughly *one third* of the amount that business had to invest to comply with governmental regulations.

The decline of private savings has been further accentuated by government policies telling people they don't *need* to worry about the future. Historically, people have saved to improve their living standards and provide for themselves in emergencies, illness or retirement. If government is going to do all these things for you, why do it for yourself? *The prime example is Social Security, which has assumed a large part of the place once occupied in future planning by personal thrift. The difference is that Social Security consists of transfer payments financed from present earnings, while the equivalent arrangement through private savings or pensions would make funds available for in-*

vestment. Harvard's Martin Feldstein has estimated the net result has been to divert as much as $61 billion a year from private savings.

Social Security, it should be added, is a prize example of a government program that started on one premise and wound up on another. When the system was launched, it was supposed to be a pay-as-you-go insurance program, supplementing retirement income at a nominal cost of $30 a year in taxes per person. Today it is a mammoth welfare program disbursing over $100 billion annually, with terrible long-term actuarial problems and a tax burden so huge that, for a majority of U.S. families, it is the largest single tax they pay.

Transfer payments from people who are working to people who are not working now amount to 53 percent of our gargantuan federal budget. This is a machine for penalizing work and rewarding idleness. Since 1969, wages and salaries in the United States have grown at an average annual rate of 9.1 percent—while transfer payments were growing at an annual rate of 14.3 percent.

In other words, we have been increasing rewards for not working at a much more rapid pace than the increase in compensation for productive labor. The result is that what little gain there has been in economic productivity in recent years has gone to recipients of transfer payments rather than to the working taxpayer.

VIII.

The Unfinished Agenda

On first appraisal, much of this book involves the topics of economics and finance. But the basic problem confronting us is actually political—more precisely, the impact of politics on our economic system, our lives, our families, our freedoms. Unless we come to terms with the political problem and free our nation from the yoke of political interference, the so-called economic questions can never be resolved.

Inflation, for example, is not an "economic issue"—it is a moral, intellectual and political issue that has devastating economic and social consequences. We must deal with it, as with our other difficulties, at the moral-political level first. We must confront the long-range implications of what we are doing to ourselves and realize that, *unless we control inflation now, we face the prospect of rampaging hyperinflation, with all the evils that entails, and a disastrous depression.*

If anything is plain from recent history, it is that the evils which beset us are not inevitable, fated in the nature of things or imposed on us by events. On the contrary, our economic collapse at home and woeful default in foreign dealings have been the result of human error and indecision, stemming from mistaken philosophies, political trimming and tunnel vision on the part of our alleged leaders.

Most of all, our gravest problems at this hour result from the power exerted over public policy by a handful of exotic theoreticians who have lost all faith in America, its traditional ideals and its future as a free society. *Driven by ideological passions, these defeatists imposed a "no-growth" posture on the United States economy and mapped out a strategy of impotence and abdication for us in our foreign dealings.*

Ridding our government of these defeatists, however, is only the bare beginnings of an answer to our problems. These ideologues were able to impose their influence on the nation because (at least until the election of President Reagan) there was a total vacuum of leadership in Washington—an aimless drift of politics as usual, devoid of principle or long-range purpose. The Reagan Administration has made a brave beginning toward recovery with its tax and budget policies, strong deregulatory initiatives and reassertion of our legitimate national interests overseas. Now it is up to all of us to build on these beginnings toward a renaissance of American strength and freedom.

It is our moral determination and our vision that define the scope of what we can accomplish; we are not determinists whose course of action is dictated by some unalterable force or by the implacable pressure of events. *We are a free people, with the power to decide our destiny. We can correct the evils that afflict us if we have the intelligence to see what must be done and the courage to take the necessary action.*

Among the most difficult changes we will have to make are those that are needed on the home front. We must restore the vitality of our economy, retool our industrial machinery, regain control of our energy destiny, lift stifling regulation, bring government spending and taxing under control and end the nightmare of runaway inflation—creating in the American people a new spirit of enterprise. In any country that has gone this far down the road to the welfare state, a reversal of the policies that have produced such evils is difficult to accomplish. But unless we do reverse them, we face the prospect of financial collapse and economic ruin. I propose a half dozen urgently needed reforms.

1. *We must bring the federal budget into balance.* The chronic something-for-nothing deficits of the past 20 years, creating massive pressures toward inflation, must be brought to a halt. The federal government must start living within its means. Allowance can be made for emergencies and for temporary deficits at times of recession, but over the course of the business cycle, the budget must be balanced. I would favor a constitutional amendment to this effect, since legislative efforts to achieve a balance have proved so totally ineffective in the past.

2. *While helping to stem the tide of inflation, a balanced budget is not a be-all and end-all in itself.* It is theoretically possible to balance the budget at 50 or 60 percent of GNP by raising taxes, which would defeat the goal of freeing our economy from the downward drag of massive government spending. It is the total burden of government that is the ultimate evil, not simply the method by which it is financed. I therefore favor a constitutional amendment to limit federal spending, placing a ceiling on total federal outlays however funded (including off-budget items, federal credits and federal loan guarantees) as a percent of GNP.

3. *We must continue to pursue the budgetary reductions that are the key to economic recovery.* The $35 billion cut voted by Congress in July 1981 was only the beginning. President Reagan has touched off anguished protests with his call for $13 billion in additional reductions, but even that is not enough. Economists for the Washington-based Heritage Foundation have identified more than $70 billion in additional savings—programs to slash, agencies to eliminate, subsidies to reduce, "uncontrollables" to at last con-

trol. Powerful interests will oppose any further economies, but they are absolutely crucial if inflation is to be conquered and crippling interest rates brought down.

4. *In keeping with a new policy of fiscal restraint, we must establish firm guidelines for the conduct of monetary policy—which has been the principal source of our runaway inflation.* In an era of double-digit price hikes, we can no longer tolerate a situation in which the supply of money grows at double the rate of GNP, sending more and more dollars in pursuit of the existing volume of goods and services. I would suggest a growth rate of two to four percent annually for the monetary base, in keeping with the long-term trend in productivity and real output.

5. *The rogue elephant of bureaucracy must be brought under control once and for all.* By his appointments and his deregulatory initiatives, President Reagan has moved to unshackle the American economy. But the power of bureaucratic agencies to serve arbitrarily and simultaneously as prosecutor, judge and executioner must be ended. And the do-it-now-and-damn-the-consequences attitude embedded in current regulatory law and the mind-set of too many regulatory bureaucrats must be curtailed. A practical rule for doing this would be obligatory "Economic Impact" or cost-benefit findings before a regulation goes into effect— and only if the benefits exceed the costs may the regulation be adopted.

6. *Literally crucial is the subject of energy. We can no longer afford to live in an energy lotusland where government holds energy prices below their market levels, yet somehow makes us "energy independent."* We need energy deregulation, mining and burning of coal, a go-ahead on nuclear power and an end to the lock-up of Alaskan and other Western lands, permitting reasonable prospecting with due regard for the environment.

Adoption of such policies would go a long way toward restoring the productive power and vibrancy of our economy, resulting in more and better jobs for American citizens, higher real incomes and an end to the silent but ruinous incursions of inflation. By reestablishing our economic vitality and ensuring the soundness of our currency, these domestic reforms would also go far toward refurbishing our tarnished image in the world arena. Additional steps are obviously needed, however, to undo the deadly peril of our current global situation.

Oddly enough, the dangers which confront us in the realm of foreign policy are, in some respects, more easily handled than those which plague us on the home front.

Not that the Soviet Union and the danger that it poses are going to fade away or that we are going to escape the rigors of the Cold War struggle at any time in the foreseeable future. *For America and its allies, the world is going to be an extremely hazardous place for many years to come.*

The steps that must be taken to shore up our ramparts against this danger, however, are relatively clear—and, given an informed public, should command a fair degree of popular support. They are clear because they are rooted in obvious common sense, outrageously flouted in the recent conduct of our foreign policy. We simply need to restore a modicum of sanity to our conduct overseas—to stop doing the criminally stupid things we have been doing to weaken our defense, destroy our allies and build up our enemies.

I will leave to those who are specialists in the strategic and technical subtleties of defense the fine points of what should be done to upgrade our military hardware. On a common-sense reading of what is happening in the world, however, and on the obvious imperatives of survival, I offer the following six-point program for the protection of our national interests and the restoration of our global leadership.

1. *We must pull our heads out of the sand of neo-isolationism, reassert our role as leaders of the free world and make the tough decisions required of leaders.* President Reagan has renounced the delusion that the Soviets are "mellowing," don't really mean it when they say they will "bury" us or somehow commit their aggressions and atrocities because we make them nervous. The grim truth is

that unless America takes the lead against the Soviets, the job will not get done. There is no one else to do it. To renounce our responsibility for this task with all that it implies in terms of human freedom, global peace and national honor is to deserve the contempt of future generations for cowardice and moral failure.

2. *We must move rapidly to repair the sagging state of our defenses, including better missiles, a new manned bomber and anti-missile defenses.* This is the one budgetary area where sharply higher spending is necessary. National survival could depend on it.

3. *The one-sided series of concessions made to Moscow in the SALT II process must never be repeated.* We can negotiate a SALT agreement, but negotiations must be from strength, not weakness, and they must be conducted on terms that protect our national security and vital interests.

4. *We must reinstitute the draft.* I was one of those who favored the experiment with the voluntary army, but I am sad to say the experiment hasn't worked. Both symbolically and substantively, the return of the draft would signal to the Russians the resolve of the American people to protect our nation's security and to bear the burden of global leadership.

5. *We must start supporting our friends and stop supporting our enemies.* The lunacy of undercutting friendly governments on the hypocritical pretext of "Human Rights"—facilitating the triumph of those who would destroy all human rights—must never be repeated. The list of former allies who have been toppled in recent years with the assistance or acquiescence of our State Department is truly appalling.

6. *We must stop building the Soviet war machine with critical infusions of our technology.* Through Orwellian illogic, we have been in the lunatic posture of creating a balance of power against ourselves—weakening our own strategic arsenal while building the economic and military strength of our opponents. Much of the threat that Moscow poses to us could be reduced if this policy were ended—

and if all commerce with the Eastern bloc were conducted on the basis of quid pro quo (such as halting the subjugation of Afghanistan). Also, we need much closer coordination with our allies to ensure that our trading policies are sensible and consistent in protecting free world interests.

In dealing with our friends, our goal should not be popularity but respect, based on firm, dependable and honest conduct. *In dealing with our adversaries, our goal should be not only respect but, in certain circumstances, fear— fear that, if aggression is committed, freedom threatened or American citizens manhandled, a swift and sure response will be forthcoming.* Only such a posture, credibly backed by the strength to enforce it, can keep the peace against aggressors.

It is not the fate of great powers to be loved or liked, and if we behave as responsible leaders in the years to come, we probably won't be very popular with the despots in the Kremlin or the "third world" noisemakers at the United Nations. Too bad. By acting with the responsible firmness and determination that befit our station in the world, however, we will be respected.

In all our affairs, domestic as well as foreign, it is a time for action—a time for renewal of the American spirit. Enterprise, thrift and self-reliance can be reborn in the United States if we adopt a plan of action based on common sense rather than on Utopian theories or childlike evasion of our duties. The long run is here, and the bills are rapidly falling due. We must face the economic facts of life. We must make the hard decisions that they require of us.

We must take the lead—with determination and with the knowledge and belief that our leadership is essential. Freedom—free people—free enterprise—a dynamic economy—is not our right, it is our privilege, if we are willing to participate and protect it.

And, with God's help, we will be free.

HOW TO ORDER MORE COPIES OF

A TIME FOR ACTION

If enough people read this best-seller by William E. Simon—and then share their new insights with others—it can change America.

Use the coupon below to order copies for your friends, your neighbors, your employees, and members of any service club or other organization to which you belong!

"A Time for Action"
NFIB Research and Education Foundation
150 W. 20th Ave.
San Mateo, CA 94403

Yes, I want more people to read *"A Time for Action,"* I understand that I can get up to 50 copies free as a public service of NFIB. Circle the number.

1   5   10   15   20   50   other____

Please send to:

_____
Name

_____
Address

_____
City   State   Zip